The Heart of Revival

The Heart of Revival manual is based on *The Heart of Revival* book
by Nicky Gumbel

First published 2000

Published by HTB Publications, Holy Trinity Brompton, Brompton Road,
London SW7 1JA

Illustrations by Charlie Mackesy

Printed in the UK by TPS Print, 5 Tunnel Avenue, Greenwich,
London, SE10 0SL
Telephone: 020 8269 1222

CONTENTS

1&2*
WHAT IS REVIVAL AND IS IT COMING?
ISAIAH 40-66

INTRODUCTION TO
ISAIAH 40-66

Revival, um, I think it's a type of drink.

1) The book of Isaiah – the Bible in miniature

* This talk covers chapters 1 and 2 in
The Heart of Revival book

Notes

Notes

2) Material in Chapters 40-66

- Crucial to our understanding of the New Testament
- Part of Jesus' self-understanding of identity and mission

3) Chapter 40
Historical background

- Israel in exile
- Sixth century
- Babylon dominant power
- Israel frustrated, depressed, bewildered cf. our own culture
- Message of exile and restoration as relevant today
- All human beings since Fall 'in exile'
- Modern Western culture 'in exile'

Message of Isaiah: 'Look up and behold your God'

Four Voices
1) LOOK, IT IS OVER (vv.1-2)

- Hard service now over
- Exile caused by sin
- Comfort – language of marriage and covenant

Lord, re. dates for revival we really feel that the 12th of June is fine

2) LOOK, GOD IS COMING (vv.3-5)

Definition of revival: 'God's manifest presence with his people'

- Human yearning for God
- God's presence is promised

3) LOOK AT GOD'S WORD (vv.6-8)

- Futility of building on temporary foundations eg money, image, property
- 'The word of our God stands for ever' (v.8)

4) LOOK AT GOD (vv.9-11)

- Transcendent – rules, rewards and recompenses
- Immanent – gentle, tender and merciful
- Cross of Christ – justice and love

Notes

Notes	Description of God in five directions

I) LOOK AT CREATION (vv.12-14)

- God made the world – beauty, intricacy and variety

II) LOOK AT THE NATIONS (vv.15-17)

- Nations come and go 'like dust on the scales'

III) LOOK AT THE IDOLS (vv.18-20)

- Absurd to worship created things eg money or sex
- Worship the one true God – the creator not the created

IV) LOOK AT HISTORY'S GREAT LEADERS (vv.21-24)

- World leaders, presidents and prime ministers pass away
- No human being can compare to God

V) LOOK AT THE STARS (vv.25-26)

- God created the stars: 100,000 million our galaxy – galaxy one of 100,000 million galaxies

Oh Jennifer, it's... it's better than match of the day..."

- God is powerful

What God wants to do

LOOK: HE IS A POWER-SHARING GOD (vv. 27-31)

- We participate in his power

Have we got right vision of God?

- Everlasting
- Full of wisdom

What are God's plans for our lives?

- To 'soar on wings like eagles'?
- To run the race with urgency
- To persevere

CONCLUSION

- Confidence that revival is coming based on God's promise: his word and character

- We have a part to play

3
WHOM WILL GOD USE?
ISAIAH 49:1-7

INTRODUCTION

Who is the servant of the Lord?
- Israel?
- Jesus Christ?
- Christians?

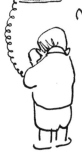

'Hello, I'd like to talk to the Arch-bishop about my future.'

'A telescopic lens on history'

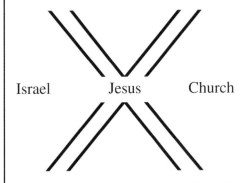

Israel   Jesus   Church

1) WE ARE CALLED TO SPEAK OUT (vv.1-2)

- Called to declare God's word
- Equipped to speak out
- Refined and purified to serve God better
- 'Hidden years' are not wasted years
  - Jesus
  - Joseph
  - Paul

2) WE ARE CALLED TO LIVE IT OUT (v.3)

- Israel failed
- Jesus fulfilled mission
- We are called to join him
- Called to demonstrate God to others – 'display my splendour' (v.3)
  - as individuals
  - the church
- Jesus perfectly reflected glory of God
- We are moving toward this (2 Corinthians 3:18)
- Allow God to work on our characters

3) WE ARE CALLED TO GO OUT (vv.4-7)

- Promise – discouragement – fulfilment
  - Abraham
  - Moses
  - Joseph
  - Jesus

Notes

- Times of testing – God rewards faithfulness, not results
- World-wide vision to 'make disciples of all nations' (Matthew 28:19)
- Progress in evangelism has been made

God glorifies the servant (v.7)

- Progress at a cost – Jesus the suffering servant
- One day every knee will bow to Jesus – voluntarily or under compulsion
- Meanwhile, tell everyone we can the good news

CONCLUSION

Huge vision

- Pray and work towards revival which extends 'to the ends of the earth'

Are we willing to

- Speak out good news?
- Live out good news?
- Go out?

All of us

- Members of church
- Can be used by God in revival

4
WHAT IS AT THE HEART OF REVIVAL?
ISAIAH 49:8 – 50:3

INTRODUCTION

The love of God

- God's covenant with Israel (v.8)
- God's unconditional love
- God's heart – moved with compassion

Five pictures of God's love

1) THE SHEPHERD (vv.9-13)

- The shepherd guides
- The shepherd protects
- Jesus is 'the good shepherd' (John 10:14)

"Eric, Janet, over here please"

2) THE PARENT (v.15)

- God's love is like that of perfect mother and father
- Impossible for God to forget his people
- Assurance that we are children of God

3) THE ENGRAVER (vv.16-23)

- 'I have engraved you on the palms of my hands' (v.16a)
- Jesus' total love and commitment seen in the nails of the cross
- Permanent and irrevocable love of God
- Promise of rebuilding and repopulation
- Triumphant return of vast numbers anticipated

4) THE CONQUEROR (vv.25-26)

- Strong and determined love of God
- God will fight our oppressors and conquer

5) THE HUSBAND (50:1-3)

- God is married to his people
- No-one out of God's reach
- We are 'the bride of Christ'

CONCLUSION

- Every revival involves a fresh understanding of God's love for us
- In every revival, the Holy Spirit is poured out
- God loves us unconditionally, wholeheartedly and continuously

5
WHAT IS THE
MESSAGE OF
REVIVAL?
ISAIAH
52:13 – 53:12

INTRODUCTION

Prophecy of the Messiah –
The fourth of the servant songs
Poem of five stanzas
First line of each gives theme
The prophet sees an extraordinary
contrast in each stanza

First contrast:
1) APPARENT FAILURE
AND ACTUAL SUCCESS
(52:13-15)

- The servant started at the
  very bottom and rose to the
  very top
- 'The cross shatters human
  expectations' Luther
- Disfigured appearance (v.14)
- The effect of suffering
  servant on all nations
- Failure - success

Second contrast:
2) OUR VIEW AND GOD'S
VIEW (53:1-3)

- Not an impressive figure in

world's terms
- Would suffer physical shame of crucifixion
- Would experience rejection by people he came to save
- Jesus continues to be rejected by those he came to save

Third contrast:
3) *OUR SIN AND HIS SUFFERING (53:4-6)*

- Jesus the supreme example of innocent suffering on behalf of guilty
- Jesus' suffering for us
- physical
- emotional
- spiritual
- Died instead of us
- Brought us peace and healing
- 'The Lord has laid on him the iniquity of us all' (v.6)

Fourth contrast:
4) *THE GUILTY AND THE INNOCENT (53:7-9)*

- Note accuracy of prophecy
- Silence in face of intense suffering
- Voluntary and undeserved death
- No retaliation
- 'Assigned a grave with the wicked' yet 'with the rich in his death'
- Joseph of Arimathea

Notes

Notes

Fifth contrast:
5) *TRAGEDY AND TRIUMPH* (53:10-12)

- Apparent defeat but in fact victory
- Cross triumph and focal point of salvation:
  - New life for millions
  - 'Light of life' a glimpse of the resurrection
  - Mission accomplished – access to God's presence for us
  - Justification – our relationship with God restored
  - Jesus lived in humility and was raised in glory

- 'He did that for me; there is nothing that I can't do for him'

CONCLUSION

- 'The point is Jesus Christ'
- Central message of revival:
  - good news of Jesus Christ
  - life, death and resurrection
- Revival comes when we understand what Jesus has done and give our lives to his service
- We should resolve to know nothing except 'Jesus Christ and him crucified'

6
WHAT IS THE VISION?
ISAIAH 54

INTRODUCTION

The world is suffering the consequences of being in exile from God

Israel compared to a woman robbed

- Of a husband
- Of her children
- Of her home

God is about to restore

- Fruitfulness
- Peace
- Righteousness

1) THE COMMAND TO GROW AND TO GO (vv.1-3)

Picture of family

Israel commanded to rejoice because God will give many children

- Get ready
- 'Strengthen your stakes' – build strong church bases
- Have more children – church plants

- Have wide vision

  - Potential is vast
  - Desperate need
  - Get message out

2) THE IMPORTANCE OF GETTING OUR PRIORITIES RIGHT (vv.4-10)

Picture of marriage (v.5)

1) Do not be afraid – most common command in Bible

- God's love restored
- God's kindness everlasting
- Eternal covenant of love and peace

2) God calls people back (vv.6-7)

- No adulterous relationships
- Our relationship with God is our number one priority
- Our ministry is secondary

16

3) THE PROMISE OF VICTORY (vv.11-17)

Picture of home and city
- reference point is rebuilding Jerusalem under Nehemiah (vv.11-12)
- application to church

God's glory will be restored to the church (vv.11-12)
- God will teach us what to do (v.13)
- God promises protection from disunity and immorality (vv.14-15)
- No attack will ultimately succeed (vv.15-17)

CONCLUSION

'Expect great things (from God), attempt great things (for God)'
William Carey

" Father, ambitious as it is, If possible, I'd like to give you a third of these toffees "

7
WHAT IS THE INVITATION?
ISAIAH 55

INTRODUCTION

'Come to me' (v.3)

'The Bible is one long invitation to come' Billy Graham

An urgent and universal invitation to those who are unsatisfied

Why should we come?

1) GOD ALONE CAN SATISFY THE HUNGER IN OUR HEARTS (VV.1-3A)

- There exists a desire that no natural happiness will satisfy – *'the real thing'* C.S. Lewis

- Invitation is to the thirsty

- Invitation is free to us but cost Jesus everything

- Those who come are deeply satisfied

2) GOD HAS A PURPOSE FOR OUR LIVES (VV.3B-5)

- David called to be 'a witness

to the peoples' (v.4)
– a 'type' of the Messiah

- Jesus = 'the one true Israelite'

- Now calling passes to us

- Called to reach every nation
  in the world

3) GREATNESS OF GOD'S LOVE AND MERCY (vv.6-9)

1) Grasp spiritual opportunities

- 'Seek the Lord while he may
  be found; call on him while
  he is near' (v.6)
- An urgency

2) Revival involves
righteousness/repentance (v.7)

- Turn away from sin
- Turn to God
- 'He will freely pardon'

3) Forgiveness greater than we can
imagine (vv.8-9)

- God's ways and thoughts are
  immeasurably higher than
  ours
- No-one too bad for forgiveness
  'No eye has seen, no ear has
  heard, no mind has
  conceived what God has
  prepared for those who love
  him'
  (1 Corinthians 2:9)

Notes

Notes

4) THE TRANSFORMING POWER OF GOD (vv.10-13)

God's word is life-changing

1) As individuals

2) For the entire creation

- We are stewards of creation
- Jesus died for creation and to defeat death
- Resurrection – a foretaste of what God will do with all creation
- In Christ, we have a place in the redemption of creation
- Creation will be set free from its bondage to decay
- A new heaven and a new earth - an everlasting sign (v.13)

CONCLUSION

We have a choice as to how we respond to God's invitation

- We can refuse
- If we accept, he will
  - satisfy the longings of our heart
  - show us the purpose for lives
  - pour out his love, generosity and transforming power
  - allow us to participate in plans for a transformed earth reflecting God's glory

8
HOW SHOULD REVIVAL AFFECT SOCIETY?
ISAIAH 58

INTRODUCTION

Christian love
Love for God and love for our
neighbour inextricably linked

1) LOVE OF GOD WITHOUT LOVE OF NEIGHBOUR (vv.1-5)

- People rebuked for privatised pietistic religion – leading to squabbling and strife
- Religious practice alongside wrong behaviour – false
- What matters – not ritual practices but obedience to God
- Obedience = love/good works

2) LOVE FOR OUR NEIGHBOUR (vv.6-12)

- Religious observance no use unless geared to needs of others
- Social responsibility for the world
- Evangelism and social action go hand in hand

Communion is AFTER the hymn. OK?

"I really feel we ought to keep fasting until our flight to Barbados comes through."

- God equips church –
  different people to different
  ministries

**What does social responsibility
involve?**

1) Social action – removal of
causes of human need (v.6)

- Three strands
  - injustice
  - inhumanity
  - inequality
- Recent history of South
  Africa
  - example of Mandela
    *'inspired a world prone to
    cynicism'*
- Examples of all three strands
  in own society eg abortion

2) Social service – direct relief of
human need (v.7)

- Three strands:
  - hunger
  - homelessness
  - poverty
- We need
  - eyes to see
  - will to act
- Can make a difference –
  think starfish!

3) Family life (v.7b)

- Possible to be socially
  sensitive and domestically

short-sighted
- Needs of own family paramount – called to build strong family life

4) Results
God's promises in response to our obedience (v.8)
- New beginning
- Restoration and healing
- Security and protection
- Answered prayer
- Light in darkness
- Guidance
- Strength
- Fresh resources (v.11b)

- Reminder: no critical attitude, gossip or slander

3) LOVE OF GOD COMBINED WITH LOVE OF OUR NEIGHBOUR (vv.13-14)

1) Consecrate life's timetable to God

2) Sabbath as symbol of wholehearted devotion to God

3) As we combine love for God and love for neighbour, promises three things

- Joy
- Confidence – 'Ride on the heights' – capacity to deal with life's problems
- Satisfaction and blessing

4) Vertical and horizontal relationships matter – Jesus demonstrates this, supremely on the cross

CONCLUSION

- True and lasting revival changes not only human hearts but communities and institutions

'The great business of the church is to reform the world - to put away every kind of sin. The Christian church was designed to make aggressive movements in every direction, to lift her voice and put forth her energies against iniquity in high and low places, to reform individuals, communities and governments, until every form of iniquity is driven from the earth'
Charles Grandison Finney (1792-1875)

9
WHAT IS THE SOURCE OF REVIVAL?
ISAIAH 61:1-11

INTRODUCTION

What does the Holy Spirit anoint us to do?

Old Testament – three levels of fulfilment

1) Foreground

- Shortly after return from exile
- Here, to a weary and disheartened people facing massive task of rebuilding

2) Middle ground

- Often at times of Jesus
- Here, hundreds of years ahead

3) Background

- Often refers to Jesus' return
- Here, God anoints us all by the Holy Spirit

Three main results of the anointing of Holy Spirit

1) WE HAVE POWER TO RESTORE THE LIVES OF INDIVIDUALS (vv.1-3)

1) Ministry = *'meeting the needs of others with the resources of God'* John Wimber

- To speak God's word
- To bring healing: physical, emotional, spiritual
- To proclaim deliverance/freedom
- To comfort all who mourn
- To plant: new life

2) WE HAVE POWER TO REBUILD THE COMMUNITY OF THE PEOPLE OF GOD (vv.4-9)

1) We are anointed by Holy Spirit

- To rebuild
- To restore
- To renew

2) The nations will co-operate (v.6)

- Material and financial support from unexpected sources

3) The church: A people blessed by the Lord (v.9b)

3) WE HAVE POWER TO AFFECT THE ENTIRE COMMUNITY (vv.10-11)

1) Picture of a wedding

- 'robe of righteousness':
  festive / undeserved
  (Romans 3:22)

2) Picture of a garden

- Righteousness and praise
  will grow 'before all nations'

3) Examples of revival affecting
wider community

CONCLUSION

Today, we need people anointed
by Holy Spirit
- To minister to people
- To rebuild the church
- To see society transformed

For revival – all need to be
anointed by power of Holy Spirit

10
HOW SHOULD WE PRAY FOR REVIVAL?
ISAIAH 62:1-7

INTRODUCTION

Our society in decline
How should we respond?

- Prayer
- Action

1) WHAT SHOULD WE PRAY FOR? (vv.1-5)

1) Prophet prays for a new righteousness (v.1)

- Righteousness - right relationship with God and each other
- Pray for genuine love in the church

2) Prophet prays for new freedom

"Apart from revival Lord, um, please - Cyril's snoring!!..

- Salvation – freedom/release from bondage

3) Prophet prays for new identity (vv.2b-4)

- Called by a new name
- A radical change in status and future
- No longer irrelevant, deserted, dwindling numbers
- Image of church today to be transformed

4) Prays for new love (vv.4b-5)

- God is committed to his people
- In response, his people are committed to him
- Picture of a wedding
- Picture of a honeymoon - new love

2) WHO SHOULD PRAY FOR REVIVAL? (v.6)

1) 'Watchmen' – prophets and intercessors

- See, hear, speak the word of God (Ezekiel 3:17)
- Watch and pray

Notes

" Sorry God, You must be tired by now, but.. "

2) All called to intercede, but some have special calling

- Pray individually and corporately for revival

3) HOW SHOULD WE PRAY FOR REVIVAL? (vv.6-7)

1) Pray constantly (v.6a)

- Contrast Isaiah 56:10 - 'Israel's watchmen lie around and sleep'
- 1 Thessalonians 5:17
- Romans 1:9-10

  - Korea – eg Dr Jashil Choi prayer mountain

2) Call on God

- Problem of invisible God
- God came down in person of Jesus
- God's love made complete in us
- 'Oh, that you would rend the

heavens and come down'
(Isaiah 64:1-2)

3) Pray with discipline
- Give yourselves no rest
- Day in, day out
- Not easy

4) Pray with urgency

- Give him no rest
- Be passionate
- Be persistent (Luke 18:1)

5) Pray with perseverance (v.7b)

- eg 1949 Hebridean revival –
  revival related to holiness

CONCLUSION

- 'A consciousness of the presence of
  God the Holy Spirit literally in
  midst of people' Dr Martyn
  Lloyd-Jones
- Definition of revival: 'a
  community saturated with
  God' Duncan Campbell

11
WHERE WILL IT END?
ISAIAH 65

INTRODUCTION

What is the meaning of history?

1) Biblical view of history = 'his story', moving to a climax

2) Climax = ultimate triumph of good and God
   - The return of our Lord Jesus Christ

How do we respond?

Here are four divisions – those who choose for God and those who choose against

1) THOSE WHO RESPOND AND THOSE WHO DO NOT (vv.1-7)

1) Jesus invited everyone but said that one day he would say to some, 'I never knew you. Away from me...' (Matthew 7:23)

2) Prophet moves to specific charges
   • Worshipping other gods – offensive to God (v.3)

- Occult practices: attempt to contact the dead (v.4)
- Disobeying God's word (v.4b)
- Spiritual pride and arrogance: attitude of superiority to others (v.5)

3) Invitation extended to all – judgement will fall on those who do not respond

2) *THOSE WHO SEEK AND THOSE WHO FORSAKE (vv.8-12)*

1) A remnant of people faithful to God – those who seek God will receive peace and overwhelming blessing from God (vv.8-10)

2) Forsakers forgot God (v.11)

- Sought 'fortune' eg today gambling
- Sought 'destiny' eg today astrology, palm-reading

3) A God of justice – solemn warning (v.12)

3) *THOSE WHO SERVE GOD AND THOSE WHO DO NOT (vv.13-16)*

1) God's servants

- They will eat, drink, rejoice and sing – every need will be met

Notes

2) The opposite for those who do not

- They will be thirsty, hungry, broken in spirit, disappointed, in anguish
- A thirst only satisfied by the presence of God

3) Servants of the Lord

- A new name: Christians (v.15)

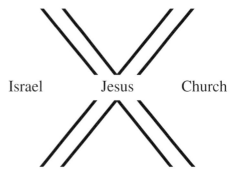

Israel   Jesus   Church

4) *THOSE ON THEIR WAY TO HEAVEN AND THOSE ON THEIR WAY TO HELL (vv.17-25)*

1) Picture of new heaven and new earth and also picture of hell

2) Nature of hell debatable, but reality certain and awful

3) Reality of heaven
'an attempt to express the inexpressible' C.S. Lewis

- A new creation (v.17)
- Incredible joy (v.18)
- No more suffering, death or pain (v.19)
- All will reach full potential (v.20)
- All activity will be a blessing (v.21)
- Closeness of relationship with God (vv.23b-24)
- Harmony and peace (v.25) - stability, safety, security, peace - total unity

CONCLUSION

A new heaven and new earth

- Need to respond to God
- Seek God
- Be his servants
- To spend all eternity with him

OTHER RESOURCES

Why Jesus?
A booklet given to all participants at the start of the Alpha course. 'The clearest, best illustrated and most challenging short presentation of Jesus that I know.' Michael Green

Questions of Life
The Alpha course in book form. In fifteen compelling chapters the author points the way to an authentic Christianity which is exciting and relevant to today's world.

A Life Worth Living
What happens after Alpha? Based on the book of Philippians, this is an invaluable next step for those who have completed the Alpha course, for anyone eager to put their faith on a firm biblical footing.

Searching Issues
The seven issues most often raised by participants of Alpha: suffering, other religions, sex before marriage, the New Age, homosexuality, science and Christianity and the Trinity.

Challenging Lifestyle
An in-depth look at the Sermon on the Mount (Matthew 5-7). The author shows that Jesus' teaching flies in the face of modern lifestyle and presents us with a radical alternative.

30 Day
Nicky Gumbel selects thirty passages from the Old and New Testament which can be read over thirty days. It is designed for those on an Alpha course and others who are interested in beginning to explore the Bible.

To order: Telephone the Alpha hotline on 0345 581278
To order from overseas: Tel. +44 1228 512 512